Spellwork

DICE

T0364065

RP Minis®
Hachette Book Group
1290 Avenue of the Americas, New York, NY 10104
www.runningpress.com
@Running_Press

First Edition: September 2023

Published by RP Minis, an imprint of Perseus Books, LLC, a subsidiary of Hachette Book Group, Inc. The RP Minis name and logo is a registered trademark of the Hachette Book Group.

The publisher is not responsible for websites (or their content) that are not owned by the publisher.

ISBN: 978-0-7624-8340-2

contents

Spellwork

DICE

Let's cast some magic, shall we, witches? When you first begin your magical practice, it can feel daunting. What type of spell do you want to cast? What do you wish to invoke? These magical dice are here to help with that. Roll them and see the foundation for a spell laid out for you.

◆ First, the **intention die** helps you figure out what spell to cast. You can always use more love, money, and protection, regardless of what's happening in your life.

◆ Second, the **magic type die** tells you what form of magic to work with, whether it's astrology or glamour magic.

◆ Third, the **magical tool die** helps you amplify your spell through methods like working with the moon phases or consulting a tarot deck.

◆ Finally, the **magical tip die** offers witch secrets to boost the power of your spell.

So go ahead, roll the dice, and manifest your dreams, witch.

DIE

① Intention

There's always a reason to cast a spell. Who doesn't want more abundance and love, even when life is going wonderfully?

Additionally, witches need to regularly integrate protection and healing work into rituals to feel like the strongest and safest versions of themselves.

LOVE:

Love is your birthright, and the romantic goddess Venus agrees. Everyone deserves to feel and give love, like the fluidity of the emotionally intelligent element water. So perform a spell to invoke love and shower yourself with romance.

PASSION:

Like love, passion is also your right. As a witch, you must escape shame to enjoy all the pleasure life has to offer. Cast a spell to invoke sensuality.

MONEY:

Witches are aware of and state their worth. You always deserve to be compensated fairly for your labor and enjoy your prosperous destiny. So cast a spell to bring monetary abundance your way.

PROTECTION:

Unfortunately, as too many witches already know, the world is not always a friendly and safe place. So, whether it be through a space-cleansing candle to rid your home of unwanted spiritual residue or a hex to protect yourself from an unwelcome ex, it's time to call upon the powers of protection.

CONFIDENCE:

Confidence is everything; it is a crucial aspect of manifestation. Never forget that you are the most essential ingredient in your magic. It can be hard to feel powerful when your self-esteem is in the gutter, so cast a spell for confidence to manifest all your desires. You deserve them.

HEALING:

Whether you're dealing with a physical ailment or an emotional or spiritual wound, you must treat yourself to self-care as healing. As a witch, you have a stash of healing tools at your disposal to help you feel your best if you allow yourself to access them.

DIE

Magic Type

Now that you know your intention, whether it be love, money, or protection, let's have fun deciding what kind of spell to cast.

    Whether you look to the night sky, consult your tarot deck, or draw yourself a magical bath, use your creativity to cast a spell directed toward your desired manifestation.

DIVINATION:

Whether you use your tarot deck, a scrying mirror, or even a crystal ball, divination is the craft of looking into the future. However, the more you practice it, the more you realize that most of the time, divination is a mirror in its own right, reflecting answers to us that we already know but may not have accepted.

ASTROLOGY:

What's your sign? By now, you should at least know your sun sign, all 12 of which come with unique traits and skillsets. Using astrology in spellwork can take many forms. First, you may wish to invoke the powers of your sign. For instance, if you're a Scorpio, the sign of death and rebirth, perhaps it's time for a spiritual makeover. However, because our complete charts contain all 12 signs, you can invoke the power of any sign you want. Tap into the seasons. For instance, use a money spell to attend a work function during Gemini season, which has a reputation for flirting, socializing, and networking with great success. You can also look to see what sign the moon body is in. For instance, when the moon is in sensual Taurus, ruled by the lover planet Venus, it could be an ideal night for a love spell.

21

KITCHEN WITCH:

The most fun part about being a kitchen witch is the food involved, but it's also a great excuse to get messy. You're already more of a kitchen witch than you think, so whether you're baking a red velvet cake infused with a marriage spell or mixing up an herbal salve to soothe muscles, express yourself and have some fun with it.

GLAMOUR MAGIC:

Beauty might be subject to societal standards and what you're born with, but glamour magic is what you make of it. Glamour includes makeup, body modifications, hair dye, and other forms of self-expression you use to feel most like yourself (and get what you want).

COLOR MAGIC:

Magical properties are associated with each color. Yellow is sunshine and joy; red is passionate love. Pink is sweet and caring love; purple is creativity and is fit for royals. Blue is protection and tranquility; green is money and abundance. Integrate color magic into your ritual, whether it's the makeup you wear or the candle you choose for a spell.

BATH MAGIC:

Did you know that your bathtub can be a giant cauldron? Treat yourself to a decadent bath filled with cleansing salts for healing and protection or petals to draw love to invoke what you desire most (while relaxing your hardworking body).

DIE

3

Magical Tool

Now that you know your intention and what kind of magic to use, let's power up your spell by adding a tool from your magical arsenal. For instance, if you're working with color magic, add a green candle to usher in abundance, and light it during the waxing moon, representing growth. Or if you're in the bath cleansing yourself of an ex, keep loving rose quartz or another crystal nearby, and light some incense for protection while you're at it. Trust your instinct and creativity to use these magical tools in a way that suits you.

TAROT:

The 78 cards offer insight as
a divination tool, but they are
also mirrors reflecting what you
already know. Tarot can provide
perspective on both professional
and personal situations. In
addition, they act as a terrific
meditation aid.

CANDLE:

To perform candle magic, first
select a candle, ideally guided
by color magic. Insert your spell
into the candle by carving sigils
into the wax or anointing the
candle with oils, available at any
occult shop, and whispering
incantations. When the candle
finishes burning, the spell
is complete.

INCENSE:

Incense sets the mood and can be found for any purpose a witch wants. For instance, use Venus incense when working with love. Keep the incense burning for clearance and protection, and let the smoke flow around your magical tools and space.

POTIONS & POWDERS:

Potions and powders can be found at your local occult store or online. Potions, such as those for love, money-drawing, or protection, can be added to candle spells or placed on the wrist or behind the ear as one would use perfume. Powders are typically sprinkled somewhere for manifestation.

For instance, thrifty powder is a money-drawing powder. Supposedly, if you sprinkle it on someone who owes you money or is being a cheapskate, it will help draw wealth your way.

CRYSTALS:

Crystals are gemstones that hold meaning. Keep crystals around your space to invoke various manifestations. For instance, rose quartz draws love, while the golden orange citrine is excellent for ushering in monetary abundance.

MOON PHASES:

The moon is an intuitive, silvery guide for all witches. Each phase corresponds with sympathetic magic properties. For example, a new moon represents fresh starts and new beginnings, a waxing moon is ideal for growth, a full moon is a potent time of culmination and manifestation,

and the waning moon is best for
protection and clearance work.

DIE

4

Magical Tip

Now, it's time to let you in on some top-secret witch tips to make your spell even more special. For instance, did you know each day of the week is associated with a planet and its properties? And if you need some extra guidance in your work, you can always call upon an ancestor or deity. Use this die to add an extra dash of sparkle to your spell.

USE THE ꝺAYS
OF THE WEEK:

In the magic world, each day
of the week is associated
with a different planet and its
properties. The intuitive moon
rules Monday, warrior Mars rules
Tuesday, chatty Mercury rules
Wednesday, lucky Jupiter rules
Thursday, lover Venus rules Friday,
strict Saturn rules Saturday, and,

as the name suggests, the bold
Sun rules Sunday.

CALL UPON AN ANCESTOR:

If you have a beloved deceased ancestor who you can call upon in times of trouble, remember that you can also pray to them while casting a spell. Sometimes a love ritual needs Grandma's blessing. You can also look to a departed figure from history or pop culture who means a lot to you.

WORK WITH A DEITY:

Sometimes, especially if you aren't close with your family, working with gods, whether it's the dark mother goddess Kali, fun-loving Dionysus, or loving Venus, can help you feel magically connected to the world around you, and your spell should improve as a result.

INVOKE THE ELEMENTS:

Earth, air, fire, and water are the four elements witches use in their practice. Integrate earth into spells for grounding and stability, air for letting go and communication, water for intuition and emotion, and fire for confidence and adventure.

CLEANSE YOUR SPACE:

Whether you're using sage, Palo Santo, or incense, get rid of any negative energy surrounding you before casting a spell to ensure protection.

ADD AN INCANTATION:

An incantation uses the ancient understanding of the power of words. Sometimes, witches prefer to practice in silence. Other times, words are needed. For instance, if you're performing a money spell, say, "This green candle I light, as it burns bright, may my bank account grow with delight."

This book has been bound using
handcraft methods and
Smyth-sewn to ensure durability.

The dust jacket and interior
were illustrated by Lively Scout
and designed by Susan Van Horn.

The text was written by
Sophie Saint Thomas.